KU-439-454

HODDER ENGLISH 4

Twelfth Night

This book guides you through each act of *Twelfth Night* in detail. Individual and group activities will help you draw out important themes and give you the opportunity to perform parts of the play as Shakespeare intended. The book will also help you prepare for coursework assignments and revision. You will develop your skills as:

SPEAKERS AND LISTENERS

by discussing the meaning of key scenes and speeches
by performing, miming and improvising parts of the play
by talking about your own ideas, experiences and opinions

READERS

by studying the play's characters, events and themes
by exploring the details of the language and its effects
by considering the historical context of the play's production in Elizabethan England

WRITERS

by writing about the play's characters, events and themes
by recording the progress of the play in a variety of note forms

ABERDEENSHIRE
BANCHORY ACADEMY
COUNCIL

ABERDEENSHIRE LIBRARIES
ABS 1981263

THE TITLE

No-one knows for sure how *Twelfth Night* came to be written, or how it got its title, though we have a number of clues. Read the information below with a partner, then use it to predict what sort of play you are about to read.

TWELFTH NIGHT (THE FESTIVAL)...

...is 6th January, and it marks the end of the traditional twelve days of Christmas. It is known as Epiphany. Many Christian families still insist that Christmas decorations can only be removed on this day.

...was a time of feasting and merry-making.

...used to be a pagan ritual which celebrated the move from the dark and cold of winter to the light and warmth of the new year.

TWELFTH NIGHT (THE PLAY)...

...was probably first shown on 6th January 1601, at Whitehall.

...among the audience at the first performance were Queen Elizabeth I and her important Italian guest Virginio Orsino.

...has an alternative title: *What You Will*.

WHAT YOU WILL

As a title, *What You Will* has a distinctive tone and can be read in a number of ways:

> Whatever you like
> Of what you dream
> Whatever you decide
> The title doesn't really matter

* Can you think of any more interpretations? Discuss the various messages which each of these readings gives you.

A portrait of Queen Elizabeth I by Nicholas Hilliard (1547–1619)

WOMEN IN LOVE: YOUR VERSION

Twelfth Night is a play about love. Love does strange things to people. What else could put us off food, make us miss a favourite television programme because we can't bear to put the phone down, or turn us into such obsessive bores that we drive our friends crazy with the sound of 'that' name?

But does gender determine the way love affects us? Do girls feel different emotions from boys? Do women react differently from men when Cupid strikes? Or are we all the same beneath the skin?

● With a partner, discuss the statements below. On a copy of the table, for each statement decide whether you agree, disagree or can't decide. Place a tick in the appropriate box.

	Agree	Disagree	Can't decide
Women need more reassurance than men.	☐	☐	☐
Men soon cool off once they've got you.	☐	☐	☐
Love matters more to men than to women.	☐	☐	☐
Women are more loyal than men.	☐	☐	☐
Sex is more important than love to men.	☐	☐	☐
Men's love is deeper and longer lasting.	☐	☐	☐
Women prefer to stick to one partner, whereas men prefer to play the field.	☐	☐	☐
Men are more concerned about appearances than what lies underneath.	☐	☐	☐
Men are more deeply affected if their lover abandons them.	☐	☐	☐
Women are taught to be more loving from an early age.	☐	☐	☐

● Compare your conclusions with others in the class. Are there any obvious differences between the opinions of girls and boys in the group? Spend some time discussing why this should be.

● What are the factors that influence our views of love? How many of these influences would have existed in Shakespeare's time? Would there have been different influences then?

As you read *Twelfth Night* you will refer back to these issues in the light of events and characters in the play. Keep your notes and return to them from time to time. And do remember – Shakespeare was male, and wrote about love from a man's point of view!

IF MUSIC BE THE FOOD OF LOVE...

As an introduction to the play, work in a group and follow the steps below:

Step 1

The opening speech of the play is delivered by Orsino, Duke of Illyria. Read the speech aloud in the following way. The first person reads up to the first slash. Allow a pause. Then the second person reads up to the second slash. Allow a pause. The third person reads up to the third slash... and so on, around the group. Read slowly. Take in the words.

> If music be the food of love, /play on;/
> Give me excess of it, /that, surfeiting,
> The appetite may sicken /and so die./
> That strain again, /it had a dying fall;/
> O it came o'er my ear /like the sweet sound
> That breathes /upon a bank of violets,/
> Stealing /and giving odour. /[*music again*] Enough; no more./
> 'Tis not so sweet now as it was before./
> O spirit of love, /how quick and fresh art thou,/
> That, notwithstanding thy capacity,
> Receiveth as the sea. /Nought enters there,/
> Of what validity and pitch soe'er,/
> But falls into abatement /and low price/
> Even in a minute. /So full of shapes is fancy,/
> That it alone /is high fantastical.

Step 2

Discuss what you have learned about the mood of Orsino from this speech. What sort of love do you think is depicted here?

Step 3

To help you to form an initial judgement about Orsino, read the statements below, and select one or two with which you most strongly agree.

Orsino strikes me as...

...a sincere and devoted lover.

...infatuated; he can think only of the object of his desire.

...jealous and resentful.

...a man falling out of love.

...a romantic who enjoys the drama of being in love.

...in pain and turmoil because of his love.

Find some evidence in the speech to support your choices, then compare your group's conclusions with those of others.

Step 4

Try to visualise what Orsino would look like. Make very brief notes on how you imagine his age, appearance and style of dress.

Step 5

Read this extract from a film screen play.

28. INTERIOR. DAY. ORSINO'S CASTLE. DRAWING ROOM
Portraits glisten in the curtained half-light. A group of military gentlemen wait patiently in various stages of boredom and frustration as an ornate piece of piano music reaches its conclusion. The impression is of a military academy. A young militarily-dressed man lies full-length on a chaise, his left hand covering his eyes, his right arm cradled in a sling, as if recovering from a battle wound. This is Orsino.

ORSINO
If music be the food of love, play on,
Give me excess of it, that, surfeiting,
The appetite may sicken, and so die.
The piano plays on to a further movement.

ORSINO
That strain again!

- How is the character of Orsino presented in this film? Why do you think he is played in this way?

- How is the text adapted to make sense of the lines?

*Toby Stephens
as Orsino, 1996*

ACT 1

Read Act 1, stopping at the end of each scene to address the key questions below.

1.1 Orsino can think of nothing but his love for Olivia, but she wants nothing to do with him.

- What is her reason?

1.2 Following a shipwreck, and her twin brother missing, Viola is washed up on the shores of Illyria. She decides to disguise herself as a young man.

- List her reasons.

1.3 Sir Toby Belch amuses himself by teasing his friend, Sir Andrew Aguecheek.

- Why does Maria tell them off?

1.4 Viola, calling herself Cesario, is now Orsino's page-boy, and has quickly gained his trust. He even sends her to woo Olivia on his behalf.

- Why does Viola find this task painful?

1.5 Olivia rejects Cesario's message from 'his' master, but finds the messenger most attractive!

- What trick does Olivia use to try to get Cesario to come back again?

ASPECTS OF LOVE

Go back over Act 1 and pick out what the characters say about the nature of love. Record these on a chart like the one below. You may wish to choose a word or two from the word bank below to describe it.

WORD BANK

sincere	unrequited	infatuated
fearful	caring	unhappy
jealous	cynical	selfish
despairing	joyful	self-love
romantic	false	brotherly
platonic	mistaken	lasting

Act & Scene	Character	What she/he says	Type of love
1.1	Orsino	'Love-thoughts lie rich when canopied with flowers'	Romantic – he is wallowing in it

Look out for the symbol as you work through this book. Add to your chart at each point.

VIOLA

Act 1 Scene 2 introduces the theme of **disguise** into the play, and triggers many of the ensuing mix-ups and complications. In it, Viola decides to dress up as a man. The disguise of Viola as a young man is central to the plot of *Twelfth Night*. Without it, there would not be much of a play. But what is in it for Viola? After all, Illyria is a man's world – a world in which a man is expected to protect his honour with his sword, and it is unlikely that Viola was given fencing lessons as a child! So why does she do it?

- Re-read Act 1 Scene 2 and try to find out why Viola disguises herself as a man.

- Make a list of the problems, sorrows and concerns which would be uppermost in Viola's mind as she sits stranded on the beach of this strange land.

- Close your eyes and think yourself into Viola's position at this point in the play. Now spend ten minutes writing a monologue (the thoughts and feelings going through Viola's head). You could start:

  Surely I will soon wake from this nightmare! Can it be true – my own, dear Sebastian drowned...?

WOMEN IN LOVE: VIOLA'S VERSION

Viola has good opportunities to compare the differences between men and women as lovers. Why?

The audience knows that she is in love with Orsino, but none of the characters on stage know this (a case of **dramatic irony** – see p23). She also has the painful task of trying to persuade Olivia to fall in love with the man she loves, and the awareness that Olivia is in love with her (as Cesario)!

It's a complicated situation. Why does Shakespeare do it? What mileage is there in it? In Act 1 Scene 5 Viola compares the effects of love on Orsino and herself. Re-read from the entrance of Viola to the end of the scene. Viola tells Olivia that Orsino loves her

With adorations, fertile tears,
With groans that thunder love, with sighs of fire.

But Viola herself says that she would love in quite a different way if she were Orsino:

Make me a willow cabin at your gate,
And call upon my soul within the house;
Write loyal cantons of contemned love,
And sing them loud even in the dead of night;

- Viola uses powerful images to illustrate the two sorts of love. Contrast these images and what they reveal about Orsino and Viola. Put into words the sort of love which each represents.

- It seems to be during this part of the play that Olivia falls in love with 'Cesario'. Discuss the qualities in Viola that really appeal to Olivia. Why is she attracted to 'Cesario' and not to Orsino?

 Add to your Love and Lovers chart.

LOCATIONS

Most of the play takes place in the houses of Olivia and Orsino. Most of the characters are seen only in the house to which they are attached, either as servant, friend or relative. However, there are a couple of characters who move from house to house and other locations.

An artist's impression of Orsino's house

An artist's impression of a location between the two houses

An artist's impression of Olivia's house

• Using a large sheet of plain paper, copy out and complete the flow chart below. This will help you to do the following:

1 keep a simple version of the complicated plot

2 track the movements of the 'mobile' characters between the two houses

3 select the most important elements of the plot.

You will need to write briefly and leave out less crucial events. Try thinking of each box as a newspaper headline.

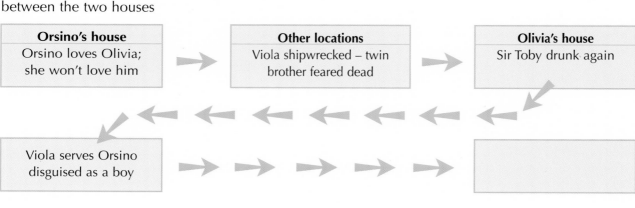

Orsino's house	**Other locations**	**Olivia's house**
Orsino loves Olivia; she won't love him	Viola shipwrecked – twin brother feared dead	Sir Toby drunk again

| Viola serves Orsino disguised as a boy | |

• Continue to record the events as you read to the end of the play.

ACT 2

Read Act 2, stopping at the end of each scene to address the key questions below.

2.1 Another sea-captain and another twin rescued from a shipwreck. This time it is Sebastian who mourns the loss of his sister, Viola.

- How do we realise the extent of Antonio's friendship?

2.2 Malvolio gives Olivia's ring to 'Cesario', adding to her confusion: she didn't leave a ring.

- How does Malvolio feel about the task he has been given?

2.3 Stung by his sharp tongue, Maria hatches a plan to bring Malvolio down a peg or two.

- What is Maria's plan? Do you think Malvolio deserves to be punished?

2.4 Orsino shares his views about love and women with 'Cesario'.

- What are they?

2.5 Maria's plan works; Malvolio takes her handwriting to be Olivia's.

- How does Shakespeare make sure that the audience is not on Malvolio's side?

'DISGUISE, I SEE THOU ART A WICKEDNESS...'

It is not too long before Viola finds that her disguise has caused a number of difficulties which she is unable to resolve. Not only has she begun to fall in love with her master, Orsino, but it seems that Olivia has taken a fancy to her. Of course, she can tell neither of them that she is really a woman. Little wonder that she declares:

O time, thou must untangle this, not I;
It is too hard a knot for me t'untie.

(Act 2, Scene 2)

On the next page is the speech which leads Viola to this outburst of frustration. It follows a conversation with Malvolio, who has been sent after Viola with Olivia's ring, saying that she had left it behind. Of course, there was no such ring, and Viola realises that Olivia has feelings for her which would embarrass them both, if the truth were known.

Imogen Stubbs as Viola, 1996

In pairs, study the speech to get a clear idea of Viola's thoughts as the realisation strikes her. Read a sentence at a time. On a separate sheet of paper, write another version in modern English. An example is given below to start you off.

Viola's soliloquy Act 2 Scene 3	
I left no ring with her: what means this lady?	*I didn't leave a ring; what is the lady up to?*
Fortune forbid my outside have not charmed her!	
She made good view of me, indeed so much That, methought, her eyes had lost her tongue, For she did speak in starts distractedly.	
She loves me sure; the cunning of her passion Invites me in this churlish messenger.	
None of my lord's ring? Why, he sent her none; I am the man;	
if it be so, as 'tis, Poor lady, she were better love a dream.	
Disguise, I see thou art a wickedness, Wherein the pregnant enemy does much.	
How easy is it for the proper-false In women's waxen hearts to set their forms!	
Alas, our frailty is the cause, not we, For such as we are made of, such we be. How will this fadge?	
My master loves her dearly, And I (poor monster) fond as much on him And she (mistaken) seems to dote on me. What will become of this?	
As I am man, My state is desperate for my master's love; As I am woman – now alas the day! – What thriftless sighs shall poor Olivia breathe?	
O time, thou must untangle this, not I; It is too hard a knot for me t'untie.	

- What is the knot that needs untangling?

- What courses of action are open to Viola? Think about them and their consequences using this chart:

VIOLA COULD...	THIS MIGHT RESULT IN...
Tell Olivia that she is really female	1. *Olivia telling Orsino* 2. 3.
Do nothing	1. 2. 3.

Now think of more options and fill them in. When you have considered all her options, decide which one you would advise her to take, and why. Compare your ideas with those of others in the class.

WOMEN IN LOVE: ORSINO'S VERSION

Have you ever wondered what the opposite sex say to each other when they discuss love and relationships? Do you think they speak differently to someone of their own sex – more honestly, perhaps? Viola is about to discover some interesting insights into Orsino's thoughts in Act 2 Scene 4.

● Here are some of the things Orsino says. Read each of these extracts carefully and then match them with the summaries given opposite.

1 *For such as I am, all true lovers are,*
   Unstaid and skittish in all motions else,
   Save in the constant image of the creature
   That is beloved.

2   *Let still the woman take*
   An elder than herself; so wears she to him;

3 *Our fancies are more giddy and unfirm,*
   More longing, wavering, sooner lost and worn,
   Than women's are.

4 *For women are as roses, whose fair flower*
   Being once displayed, doth fall that very hour.

5 *There is no woman's sides*
   Can bide the beating of so strong a passion
   As love doth give my heart; no woman's heart
   So big, to hold so much.

6   *[Women] lack retention.*
   Alas, their love may be called appetite,
   No motion of the liver, but the palate,
   That suffers surfeit, cloyment, and revolt,
   But mine is all as hungry as the sea,
   And can digest as much.

a Our feelings are more changeable than women's are.

b Women have smaller hearts, so they cannot love as deeply as men.

c The true lover's feelings may change toward many things, but never toward the image of the beloved.

d Women have a smaller appetite for love; they soon get bored of it. But there is no limit to my appetite for love.

e A man should choose a woman younger than himself, so that over time she will grow to suit him.

f A woman's beauty is like the rose; it quickly fades.

● Sum up Orsino's attitudes to women in your own words.

● Now imagine Viola were asked to complete the exercise you were given on page 3, expressing her agreement or disagreement with each of Orsino's statements above. What would she say to each one?

  Add to your Love and Lovers chart.

READING BETWEEN THE LINES

During the conversation between Orsino and Viola about the differences between men and women in love, Viola is obviously frustrated because she cannot say what she really feels (and must not reveal her feelings toward Orsino!)

Reread the conversation. Look carefully at the passage and, on a separate sheet, make notes to show what Viola is thinking and what she would like to say if she could.

Orsino Make no compare
Between that love a woman can bear me
And that I owe Olivia.

Viola Ay, but I know–

Ay, but I know how much a woman can be in love because...

Orsino What dost thou know?

Viola Too well what love women to men may owe.
In faith, they are as true of heart as we.
My father had a daughter loved a man
As it might be, perhaps, were I a woman,
I should your lordship.

I know only too well that women can love as true as men. I am...

Orsino And what's her history?

Viola A blank, my lord. She never told her love,
But let concealment, like a worm i' th' bud
Feed on her damask cheek. She pined in thought,
And with a green and yellow melancholy
She sat like Patience on a monument,
Smiling at grief. Was not this love indeed?
We men may say more, swear more, but indeed
Our shows are more than will: for still we prove
Much in our vows, but little in our love.

Concealing my love from you, Orsino, is almost unbearable. It feels like...

Orsino But died thy sister of her love, my boy?

Viola I am all the daughters of my father's house,
And all the brothers too – and yet I know not.
Sir, shall I to this lady?

I am that sister! And my brother...

Orsino Ay, that's the theme.
To her in haste; give her this jewel; say
My love can give no place, bide no denay.

In your notes, you should aim to bring out the differences between what Orsino and Viola say and what they really think. In a group, compare your comments with those of others so that you can look at alternative ideas. What does Act 2, Scene 4 say about disguise?

 Add to your Love and Lovers chart.

SPORT ROYAL: THE GULLING OF MALVOLIO

In Act 2 Scene 5 we see the outcome of Maria's plan to trick Malvolio into believing that Olivia is in love with him. Malvolio has found the letter purporting to be from Olivia, and, as Maria's handwriting is so similar to Olivia's, believes it to be genuine. As he works to interpret the meaning of it, he becomes more and more excited by what it seems to reveal. Of course, he does not realise that he is being spied on by Sir Toby and friends, and so he doesn't try to hide his true feelings. In this way, the audience learns a lot about Malvolio's character. The success of the scene depends on the audience seeing and hearing what Malvolio cannot.

Using the guidelines below, devise a class mini-production of the scene.

IN GROUPS...

- Work in groups of six. Five of you take the parts of Maria, Sir Toby, Sir Andrew, Fabian and Malvolio. The sixth person will be the director.

- Divide the scene up so that each group is responsible for presenting a section of maybe thirty lines (this will depend on the size of the class).

- Read your section several times. Remember: the audience can see and hear all the characters – but Malvolio thinks he is alone.

- Agree on the most significant event in your section. It is this which you must convey to the audience.

- Using your director to 'mould' you, produce a 'still image' (see the Help Box below) to depict the position of each character at the start of your section. You should exaggerate the body language and facial expressions. Show where each character is positioned in relation to Malvolio. Practise holding your position for at least fifteen seconds.

- Now produce another 'still image' to depict the end of your section.

- Select the most important line or two. Decide as a group how it should be spoken, using your director to guide you. The person whose line it is should learn it by heart and say it aloud.

- Now put your sequence together: freeze frame – spoken lines – freeze frame.

HELP

Still image – sometimes called a 'freeze frame' or 'tableau'. Characters take up position as if the camera caught the act. It can be 'brought to life' if necessary or characters asked to speak aloud what they are thinking at that moment. This will reveal the relationships between the characters.

[continued over...]

Beerbohm Tree as Malvolio, 1901

Stephen Lewis as Malvolio at the Young Vic, 1983

Richard Durden as Malvolio at the Nottingham Playhouse, 1995

AS A CLASS...

- Watch each group's presentation in turn, so that you see the whole scene in its correct sequence.

- Now try to watch the scene as a video film.

AS A FOLLOW ON YOU MIGHT LIKE TO...

- Use a camera to take still photographs of each still image.

- Make a storyboard of the photographs to display on the classroom wall. Support each pair of photographs with your chosen quotation.

ACT 3

Read Act 3, stopping at the end of each scene to address the key questions below.

3.1 Olivia confesses her love to 'Cesario'.

- What might be her hopes and fears at this point in the play?

3.2 Sir Andrew is jealous of 'Cesario', so Sir Toby encourages him to challenge 'Cesario' to a duel.

- Why does Sir Toby do this?

3.3 Sebastian and Antonio have reached Illyria. Antonio is unable to enter the city.

- What reasons does he give?

3.4 Olivia is astonished when Malvolio acts on the instructions in the letter, and has him locked up as a madman. The duel goes wrong when Antonio appears and draws his sword on 'Cesario's' behalf, taking him for Sebastian. Antonio is arrested.

- How does Viola gain new hope from this incident?

SHAKESPEARE'S THEATRE

You may have learned about Shakespeare's theatre in previous studies. Read carefully the points opposite about the workings of the Elizabethan theatre. The way in which plays were performed in Elizabethan times has a special bearing on *Twelfth Night*.

An artist's impression of the Globe Theatre in Shakespeare's time

Women were not allowed to act in Shakespeare's time. The female parts were taken by young boys before their voices broke.

- This could be a nuisance, but how does Shakespeare turn it to his advantage in this play?

Plays were presented in the afternoon, in broad daylight with virtually no set, and just a few props.

- How does Shakespeare overcome the problem of setting the time, place and mood? Find some examples of Shakespeare doing this.

- Can you think of any advantages in having little or no set?

Hundreds of people stood throughout the performance by buying cheap tickets for the standing area by the stage. The plays were long and demanded concentration.

- How does Shakespeare keep up the pace and interest level of the play?

- How does he build in breaks to avoid overloading the audience with serious and intense scenes?

There were two doors in an Elizabethan theatre: one at each side of the stage. Between them was a small recess, concealed by a curtain. Above was a balcony.

- Can you see any use for these features in *Twelfth Night* so far?

A standing spectator's view of the stage at the new Globe Theatre today. The theatre was rebuilt to match the original Globe Theatre as closely as possible. It opened in 1997.

'BY MAIDHOOD, HONOUR, TRUTH, AND EVERYTHING'

In Act 3 Scene 1, Olivia can contain her love no longer, and confesses it to 'Cesario'.
This is a painful admission for Olivia for a number of reasons:

- She has foresworn men for seven years in order to mourn her dead brother
- 'Cesario' is a servant, and she is a lady
- 'Cesario' has given no clear signals that he returns her feelings
- She is having to make the first move.

Read these two speeches. The first is Olivia's confession, the second is Viola's reply.
Annotate the two speeches, considering the questions below.

Olivia

Cesario, by the roses of the spring,
By maidhood, honour, truth, and everything,
I love thee so that, maugre all thy pride,
Nor wit nor reason can my passion hide.
Do not extort thy reasons from this clause,
For that I woo, thou therefore hast no cause;
But rather reason thus with reason fetter:
Love sought is good, but giv'n unsought is better.

Viola

By innocence I swear, and by my youth,
I have one heart, one bosom, and one truth,
And that no woman has; nor never none
Shall mistress be of it, save I alone.
And so, adieu, good madam; never more
Will I my master's tears to you deplore.

- What signs are there that Olivia's feelings are sincere and heartfelt? Think about:

  what she swears by

  the words she uses

  the use of rhyme and rhythm.

- Can you find any ways in which Viola's speech picks up, or echoes, the style of Olivia's?

- The use of rhyming couplets, where pairs of lines rhyme on their last words, is uncommon in Shakespeare's plays. Read each speech aloud with a partner to see how it sounds.

- Think about other forms of writing you have come across which use rhyming couplets. What type of writing do you associate with this form?

- What effect do you think the use of rhyming couplets has on the mood and style of what is said? How different would the speeches be in prose? Or in blank verse?

Add to your Love and Lovers Chart.

THE SERVANT'S HALL

Working in small groups, imagine you are servants to Olivia and Orsino. Naturally, you have been taking an interest in the goings-on between your employers and their households. It may even be that some of you have 'accidentally' overheard private conversations whilst going about your duties!

- Agree on a location at which you might meet together (for instance, at the inn on your night off, or in the servants' hall of one of the houses while delivering goods or messages.)

- Think about the characters you are to play and make notes, for example:
  Robert
  15 years old
  stable lad
  works for Olivia

- Role-play the conversation which might take place, commenting on the antics of your employers, particularly their love-lives and the local gossip. Then act out your conversations to the rest of the class.

- Write a similar conversation as a playscript. You could begin:

Matthew *(groom to Olivia)*	My poor mistress has not been herself since the death of her brother. She takes no interest in the horses any more, but just moons around looking miserable...
Curio *(Gentleman to Orsino)*	Funny you should say that, because Orsino...

'THEY WILL KILL ONE ANOTHER BY THE LOOK, LIKE COCKATRICES'

Much of the humour in *Twelfth Night* arises from the deliberate attempts by Sir Toby Belch and his cronies to amuse themselves at the expense of other characters. Sir Andrew Aguecheek is an easy target, who is deceived by Sir Toby through much of the play into believing that he stands a chance of winning Olivia's hand in marriage.

Look at the episode in Act 3 Scene 4, in which Sir Toby engineers a sword-fight between Sir Andrew Aguecheek and 'Cesario'. Now read the letter in which Sir Andrew writes to 'Cesario', challenging him to a duel. You will find this on the next page.

Youth, whatsoever thou art, thou art but a scurvy fellow.

Wonder not, nor admire not in thy mind, why I do call thee so, for I will show thee no reason for it. Thou com'st to the Lady Olivia, in my sight she uses thee kindly; but thou liest in thy throat, that is not the matter I challenge thee for.

I will waylay thee going home, where if it be thy chance to kill me—thou kill'st me like a rogue and a villain.

Fare thee well, and God have mercy upon one of our souls! He may have mercy upon mine, but my hope is better, and so look to thyself.
Thy friend, as thou usest him, and thy sworn enemy,

Andrew Aguecheek

- How much evidence does the letter contain to suggest that Sir Andrew is a fearsome and accomplished swordsman? How would you describe the tone and style of this letter?

- What is Viola to make of this? She has obviously offended Sir Andrew in her disguise as Cesario, but how?

Were Viola really the fit young man she appears to be, this would leave her more bemused than terrified. She would probably share Fabian's view of the letter:

'Very brief, and to exceeding good sense [Aside] – less.'

There is not much fun in this for Sir Toby, so he decides not to deliver the letter, but to tell 'Cesario' of the challenge verbally. This will give him the chance to exaggerate Sir Andrew's fierceness! So this is the report of Sir Andrew that 'Cesario' receives:

'He is a knight, dubbed with unhatched rapier, ... a devil in private brawl. Souls and bodies hath he divorced three, and his incensement at this moment is so implacable that satisfaction can be none but by pangs of death and sepulchre... Therefore on, or strip your sword naked; for meddle you must, that's certain, or forswear to wear iron about you.'

Little wonder that Cesario protests, 'I am no fighter'. But far from reporting this response to Sir Andrew, Sir Toby carries back this description of the trembling Viola:

'Why, man, he's a very devil... They say he has been a fencer to the Sophy*... he will not now be pacified. Fabian can scarce hold him yonder.'

* a ruler of Persia in the 16th–17th centuries.

- Imagine that the play were to be updated to modern times, using modern English and contemporary images. Re-write each of the extracts above, aiming to make each opponent sound as terrifying as possible.

- What do you now make of Sir Toby's declared aim that,

  'This will so fright them both that they will kill one another by the look, like cockatrices*.'?

* According to legend, the cockatrice was a monster so fearful in appearance that anything it looked upon would die of fright.

HELP

This is a fine example of **dramatic irony**. Dramatic irony occurs when the audience of a play knows more than the characters and can predict comic results before they happen. Here, Sir Andrew and Viola are shaking in their boots, but the audience recognises that the descriptions which they have been given are very far from the reality. Compare the gulling of Malvolio in Act 2, Scene 5.

ACT 4

Read Act 4, stopping at the end of each scene to address the key questions below.

4.1 Sebastian is mistaken for 'Cesario' by a number of people, including Olivia, with whom he agrees to go home.

- Why would this surprise Olivia?

4.2 Feste torments Malvolio, but finally agrees to take a letter from him to 'Cesario'.

- Whose decision is it to end the trick?

4.3 Olivia and Sebastian are betrothed to be married.

- Why doesn't Shakespeare end the play here?

'YET 'TIS NOT MADNESS': OLIVIA AND SEBASTIAN

Re-read Act 4, Scene 3 in which Olivia and Sebastian 'plight their troth' but agree to keep their engagement secret for the time being. Olivia, of course, believes that Sebastian is Cesario, whom she has loved for some time. Sebastian, on the other hand, is a stranger to Illyria and has only just met Olivia.

- Below are some of the things Sebastian says in this scene. Read each extract carefully. Then, on a separate sheet, jot brief notes alongside each one describing the character's state of mind at this point.

Sebastian says	I think
This is the air, that is the glorious sun...	*He is feeling high on love.*
And though 'tis wonder that enwraps me thus, Yet 'tis not madness	
My soul disputes well with my sense That this may be some error...	
...flood of fortune	
Or else the lady's mad;...	
...yet if 'twere so, She could not sway her house, command her followers, Take and give back affairs and them dispatch, With such a smooth, discreet, and stable bearing As I perceive she does.	
I'll follow this good man, and go with you, And having sworn truth, ever will be true.	

- Having looked at the evidence, what do you consider to be Sebastian's motives in agreeing to the betrothal? Is it because:

he needs a home?   it's a case of love at first sight?   he's mad?

he is bewitched?   he's afraid of offending Olivia?   he thinks she's mad?

Now repeat the activity focusing on Olivia to gain an insight into her state of mind.

Olivia says	I think
Blame not this haste of mine.	
...If you mean well, Now go with me, and with this holy man...	
Plight me the full assurance of your faith, That my most jealous and too doubtful soul May live at peace.	
... heavens so shine, That they may fairly note this act of mine!	

- Why is Olivia so keen to rush them both into this betrothal? Think about all that has passed between Olivia and Cesario (whom she believes Sebastian to be) until this point.

- And finally, is this true love for Sebastian and Olivia?

Add to your Love and Lovers chart.

ACT 5

Read Act 5 and address the key questions below, before moving on to activities about the whole play.

5.1 Antonio is taken before Orsino.

Olivia mistakes 'Cesario' for Sebastian.

Orsino thinks 'Cesario' has betrayed him.

Andrew Aguecheek and Toby Belch are slightly wounded in a sword fight after mistaking Sebastian for 'Cesario'.

Viola's true identity is revealed, and Orsino proposes to her.

Malvolio is released.

- Why so much action but only one scene? All the other acts in the play consist of between three and five switches of scene. With a partner, try to divide Act 5 up into three or four convenient sections. You will need to look for breaks in the plot.

Why do you think Act 5 was not divided into scenes when the others were?

ENDINGS

- What do you expect from happy endings? Write a list of the things that conventionally happen to:

  People in love
  People who are not loved in return, even at the end
  People who are lost or separated
  People who are vain, cruel, stupid or unpleasant in some way
  Rich and powerful people
  Poor and powerless people
  Heroes and villains
  Complications
  Confusions and misunderstandings
  Money

- Who is rewarded in *Twelfth Night,* and with what?

- Who is punished in *Twelfth Night,* and with what?

- For whom has nothing changed at the end of *Twelfth Night* and why?

- Is the world a better place at the end of *Twelfth Night*? In what ways?

COMEDY

- Think about jokes, programmes and people who make you laugh. What examples of comedy can you think of under these headings?

Play on words

Mistaken identity

'Over the top' behaviour

Making fun of other people

Slapstick

Practical jokes

Deception (lies and trickery)

Satire (ridiculing famous people or events)

- Can you think of other types of humour?

- What examples can you think of in *Twelfth Night*? What are Shakespeare's favourite types of comedy in this play?

Several of Shakespeare's plays are called 'Comedies' and *Twelfth Night* is one of them. The idea of 'comedy' goes back in time as far as Ancient Greece and has been used and re-interpreted in many ways throughout the history of literature. There are particular elements which 'comedies' have in common.

A COMEDY...

...has an elaborate plot involving misunderstandings and deceptions

...begins with the possibility of disaster which is then happily resolved at the end (often symbolised by a wedding)

...does not concentrate on the fortunes of an individual, but of a group of people

These conventions are not strict rules. In *Twelfth Night*, can you think of any elements which are not comic?

FESTE

'I am indeed not her fool, but her corrupter of words.'

Feste is known as the 'fool' but he is obviously far from foolish! Here are some of the things that people have said about Feste:

• Read each statement and discuss it with a partner, deciding which ones you agree with.

Feste is employed to provide entertainment with witty word play, jokes and music.

Feste is there to make other characters look clever.

Feste is there to make other characters look stupid.

Words of wisdom are delivered by Feste in a light-hearted manner.

Like Viola, Feste moves between the houses of Olivia and Orsino, providing an important link in communications.

Feste is the voice of caution in the play – he observes the lovers cynically and does not set much store by love and marriage.

He's really just a servant.

Feste is the Elizabethan equivalent of a TV comedian, there to provide a little escapist entertainment.

• Find examples to illustrate each of the statements with which you agree.

FESTE'S SONGS

Music is one of the main themes in the play, and is usually linked with love. Remember Orsino's opening lines: 'If music be the food of love, play on...' (Act 1, Scene 1).

As well as expressing moods of love, music also lightens the more serious scenes and reminds the audience that this is comedy. Feste's songs do both of these things, by making serious points about the events on stage.

Here is the song that Feste sings in response to Sir Toby's request for a love song.

O mistress mine, where are you roaming?
O stay and hear, your true love's coming,
  That can sing both high and low.
Trip no further, pretty sweeting;
Journeys end in lovers meeting,
  Every wise man's son doth know.

What is love? 'Tis not hereafter;
Present mirth hath present laughter:
  What's to come is still unsure.
In delay there lies no plenty,
Then come kiss me, sweet and twenty:
  Youth's a stuff will not endure.

(Act 2 Scene 3)

- What is the 'message' in the poem? Why is it relevant at this point in the play?

- Read the songs in Act 2 Scene 4 and at the end of the play. What do they add to the play besides a musical break?

- Why do you think Shakespeare chose to end the play with a song? And why that song?

John Laurie as Feste and Phyllis Neilson-Terry as Olivia at the New Theatre, 1932

CHARACTER RESEARCH

- Divide the main characters up among the class so that each group is responsible for a different character. Look back through the play to find scenes in which your character features. Your group's aim is to find out as much as you can about your character and later to pass your findings on to the rest of the class. Use the following headings to guide your research:

  background and position in Illyrian society

  his or her personality

  his or her role in the story

  how others see them

  important things they say

  his or her view of love

  how they are rewarded, punished or changed at the end of the play.

- Under each heading collect a list of points with quotes or examples to illustrate them. When your notes are complete, produce a mini-poster to share with the rest of the class by photocopying it and presenting it to them.

- Explain your poster to the rest of the class, and listen carefully to what other groups have to say about their characters. What similarities or contrasts begin to emerge?

- If there is space, display your posters on the wall so that you can all have a good look at how each character is represented.

LOVE IS...

The poem 'Love is...' by Adrian Henri takes a humorous look at what love means to different people. Read these extracts from it several times:

LOVE IS...

Love is feeling cold in the back of vans
Love is a fanclub with only two fans
Love is walking holding paintstained hands
Love is

Love is the presents in Christmas shops
Love is when you're feeling Top of the Pops
Love is what happens when the music stops
Love is

Adrian Henri

- What images come to your mind when you think about what love means to you? Use them to add a further verse to the poem describing your ideas about what 'Love is...'.

- Now choose one of the main characters from *Twelfth Night* and write a verse or two of 'Love is...' as though you were your chosen character. Plan this activity by looking carefully at the sort of events and language associated with your character. You may find your Love and Lovers chart useful here.

- Read your finished poem aloud to the class, without revealing which character you wrote as. See if they can guess your character.

Ben Kingsley as Feste, 1996

IDEAS FOR WRITTEN WORK

The following questions will give you opportunities to revise and develop what you have learned in this book. Alternatively, any of them could be used as a starting point for a piece of course work on *Twelfth Night*.

- What would be Viola's thoughts and feelings at the end of the play? Write as though you are Viola perhaps as a monologue describing her adventures in Illyria. You should think about:

  her reunion with Sebastian

  Sebastian's marriage to Olivia

  her own relationship with Orsino

  what it is like to live as a man!

- It is said that *Twelfth Night* was written to provide a little light-hearted entertainment to cheer the audience in the depths of winter. However, it does have a number of serious things to say. How is comedy used to say them? To help you with this question you might:

  look at the lessons characters learn from tricks played on them

  consider the role of Feste

  find examples of humour which reveal something about human nature.

- Compare and contrast the various types of love which are presented in *Twelfth Night*. In your opinion, who are the most sincere lovers? Consider:

  romantic love, sibling love, platonic love...

  how the lovers are tested, and how they respond

  which of the romantic relationships would be most likely to endure.

- In what ways is *Twelfth Night* a play designed for the Elizabethan theatre? What are the implications for producers today? Consider:

  the use of gender changes

  the use of the stage area

  the skills demanded of actors

  its appeal to a mixed audience

  its themes and how well they have stood the test of time

  the language and how well it has stood the test of time.